A Brief Read

Of

And the Mountains Echoed

by

Khaled Hosseini

A Summary

by

Kajal Nair

A Brief Read

Do you love to read, but don't have the time? Do you wish you could read every book on the best sellers list? Can you afford every book on the best sellers list?

The A Brief Read series is for you! Every year, over two million books are published, but there is never enough time and money to read them all.

Each A Brief Read book is approximately 25 to 35% of the length of the original book. Our writers strive to retain the story line, suspense, and overall feel of the original book, but you can read it in a quarter of the time! You will recognize A Brief Read Summaries by their well developed characters and quick pace.

If you enjoy the story, you might even work in some time to read the original. If there's a book that you'd like to see in A Brief Read, let us know!

Table of Contents

About the Author

Introduction

Chapter 1

Chapter 2

Chapter 3

Chapter 4

Chapter 5

Chapter 6

Chapter 7

Chapter 8

Chapter 9

Final Recap

Critical Review

About the Author

Born in Afghanistan in 1965, Khaled Hosseini moved to the United States to work as a physician. He made his debut as a writer in 2003 with his bestselling novel, *The Kite Runner*. This was followed by *A Thousand Splendid Suns. And the Mountains Echoed* is his third book.

Hosseini's novels are Afghan-centric, with most of his characters being Afghani, but his stories touch on universal topics like family, love, and loss. Hosseini claims that much of his inspiration for his novels comes from his childhood days in Afghanistan.

The Khaled Hosseini Foundation provides humanitarian assistance to Afghanistan. Hosseini lives in North Carolina with his wife and two children.

Introduction

Out beyond ideas of wrongdoing and rightdoing,

There is a field. I'll meet you there.

These lines from a Rumi poem aptly form the epigraph of *And the Mountains Echoed.* At the heart of it, this book explores the fine line between right and wrong, pushing readers to question the various shades of human nature.

A complex tale that weaves through several generations and continents, Khaled Hosseini once again delivers a story about the fragility of human relationships. The story moves back and forth, from Afghanistan to California to Greece and France.

The reader follows the lives of several characters as they make choices that resonate across the globe and through generations. Hosseini explores human flaws and touches on the topics of family, love, honor, betrayal, and sacrifice.

The story begins in a small village in Afghanistan. Abdullah and his sister, Pari, share an extraordinary bond and a painful choice tears them apart. The separation of the siblings sets the foundation of this sweeping tale which reads like a series of intertwined short stories.

And the Mountains Echoed is an unforgettable novel that becomes more powerful with each page, evoking a range of emotions from the reader.

Chapter 1

Fall 1952

Abdullah and Pari sat in rapt attention as their father, Saboor, told them a story. It was late into the night and Pari had to leave with her father early the next morning. It was going to be a long day, but little Pari and Abdullah insisted on a story before going to bed. They looked forward to these stories that always transported them to the enchanted world of *divs* and *jinns.*

"Once upon a time, there was a farmer named Baba Ayub in the small village of Maidan Sabz. Years of drought had made life a struggle for the village inhabitants.

Baba Ayub worked hard every day to provide for his family. He loved his wife dearly. He was blessed with three sons and two daughters who meant the world to him. Even though he would never openly admit it, Baba Ayub had a special fondness for his youngest, three-year-old son, Qais.

Qais was a charming little boy, but as a child he developed a sleepwalking problem. His parents were worried and tried every trick in the book, but nothing seemed to work. Eventually, Baba Ayub thought of an ingenious plan. He found a tiny bell and tied it around Qais' neck. The bell would jingle and wake someone up every time Qais started to sleepwalk in the night.

The sleepwalking stopped in due time, but Qais developed an attachment to the bell and refused to take it off. Every evening, when Baba Ayub returned home, Qais would run into his father's arms, the bell jingling with every step he took.

Alas, this family's happiness was short-lived. One day a *div* came to Maidan Sabz. As the *div* entered the village with thundering footsteps, the villagers locked themselves in their houses. They trembled with fear for they knew what was going to befall them.

They had heard stories of the *divs* visits to other villages. The *div* would tap on the roof of a house. When it did so, the family would be forced to give away one of their children. No one would ever see the child again. If a family refused to give one child, the *div* would take away all of the children in the family.

The div took the children to its fort, on a steep mountain. Getting there required days of journey through vast expanses of deserts and mountains. The fort was a labyrinth of dungeons with meat hooks hanging from the ceiling. No trespasser ever survived as they would be eaten by the *div*.

That day, the *div* knocked on the roof of Baba Ayub's house. Baba Ayub let out a heart wrenching cry as he heard the knock. He had one night to make a decision. The *div* would be back for a child at sunrise. No parent should ever be forced to make such a choice. Baba Ayub and his wife spent an agonizing night, whispering to each other, helpless and lost. The night wore on and as dawn approached, Baba Ayub and his wife were still unable to make a decision. They couldn't possibly choose one child to give away to the div.

In desperation, Baba Ayub picked up five stones and wrote the name of a child on each stone. He asked his wife to pick a stone and she did so reluctantly, knowing that she didn't have a choice. They had to give up one child to save the others. The stone his wife pulled out had Qais' name on it. On reading his youngest son's name, Baba Ayub screamed out in anguish.

It was almost sunrise and Baba Ayub picked up his child and placed him outside the house, closing the door behind him. Baba Ayub began weeping uncontrollably as he heard his little child pounding on the door and then the *div's* thunderous footsteps and Qais' screams, until there was nothing left but silence.

Years passed and Baba Ayub's sorrow seemed to multiply and expand with each passing day. The drought in the village worsened, but Baba Ayub was incapable of doing anything to provide for his family. He'd sit at the edge of his farm and stare at the mountains for hours

One day, Baba Ayub left his house at dawn, while his children and wife were still sleeping. He walked tirelessly for days, surviving on wild berries, mushrooms, and fish. His feet would bleed and he would go for days without food, but nothing could stop him. He walked endlessly, until he reached the *div's* fort.

Baba Ayub encountered the *div* as the gates of the fort creaked open. He was fearless as he drew his scythe. He had nothing to lose anymore, "You took my dearest child away from me. I'm here for revenge."

"I admire your courage," the *div* replied, undaunted by Baba Ayub's declaration, "I'll grant you a duel, but first you'll have to follow me."

Baba Ayub followed the *div* with reckless abandon through a maze of chambers and stairwells. Finally, they entered an enormous room at the end of which was a curtain. The div pulled back the curtain and Baba Ayub found himself looking through the window at a beautiful garden. He watched children running and chasing each other in the garden and noticed Qais among them. Relief washed over him. His son was alive!

"This was a test of your love. You came here, so you have passed," the div explained, "Had you failed the test, all of your children would die, cursed as they were to be fathered by a coward. Your son does not remember you. He is happy here. He receives a good education and there is nothing that he wants for. When he reaches adulthood, he'll be free to leave this place."

"I want to take him home," Baba Ayub said meekly.

"Do you, really? You're free to take him, but what kind of life would you be able to provide for your son?"

It was a heart-breaking decision, but Baba Ayub chose to leave without his son. The *div* was right. He didn't want to take his son back to the drought-stricken village after seeing the life that had been offered to him.

As Baba Ayub left the fort, the *div* handed him a glass flask filled with a liquid. He asked Baba Ayub to drink the liquid before he got home.

When Baba Ayub returned to his village, he remembered nothing of his journey. What's more? He couldn't recollect that he ever had a son named Qais. This was the *div's* reward, to relieve Baba Ayub of any memories of losing a child.

That year, the rains fell with all their glory in the village of Maidan Sabz. The village would never suffer from drought again, and Baba Ayub's family prospered. He grew old and watched his children marry and have several children of their own.

Sometimes, in moments of silence, Baba Ayub would hear a sound, like the jingling of a bell. He would never understand where the noise came from and what it meant. But each time he heard it, he would look around in surprise, expecting to see something or someone. These moments passed, and after they did, Baba Ayub never gave it much thought.

He lived the rest of his life surrounded with happiness and love, not knowing of the existence of his youngest son."

Chapter 2

Fall 1952

Saboor whacked Abdullah on the side of his head.

"Go home," Saboor said. Abdullah had been following the red wagon which Saboor and Pari had taken off in early that morning. His antics made Saboor furious.

Pari broke into tears, as her father returned back to the wagon, leaving the little boy behind. But Abdullah was relentless. He kept following the wagon, unwilling to leave his sister.

He was supposed to stay back home, in Shadbagh, with Saboor's wife, Parwana, and Abdullah's younger half-brother, Iqbal. Abdullah refused to leave his sister's side. Their father eventually gave up and allowed his son to follow them. The journey to Kabul was going to be a long, tiring one. Nabi, Saboor's brother-in-law, had offered to drive them. Saboor chose, instead, to walk the entire way, dragging along the wagon, on the bed of which little Pari sat. Her tears had dried up, now that she knew her brother was coming with them.

Pari's eyes suddenly lit up as she pointed towards something lying on a boulder. It was a feather. Pari had always had a strange fascination for feathers, and she collected them in an old tin tea box that her brother had given her. Abdullah picked up the long, grey feather and handed it to her.

Pari's most prized possession was a striking green peacock feather. It had been a gift from her brother. Abdullah had heard about a boy from another village whose family owned a peacock. He ended up giving away his shoes in exchange for a single peacock feather. He had walked home with bloodied feet.

By the time he reached Shadbagh, it was late in the evening. He walked around the hut to avoid his step-mother, Parwana, who was busy making bread before the *tandoor,* and tiptoed to where Pari lay sleeping. As he presented Pari with the beautiful feather and watched her pretty face light up, he knew that it had all been worth it. Pari meant the world to her ten year old brother. She was his only real family.

Their mother had died three and a half years ago, while giving birth to Pari. Abdullah was only seven then, but he took responsibility for his sister while their father worked and mourned the loss of his beloved wife. Abdullah had always been more parent than brother to his sister, and they both loved each other deeply.

Saboor remarried and brought Parwana into their lives. She was always gentle with Abdullah and Pari, sewing clothes and making them dolls. Her patience and gentleness with the kids came to her naturally since she had spent years caring for her invalid sister. Abdullah knew that these were just acts. Parwana would never, could never, love the two of them like one would love their own child. He longed for his mother. The love that a mother had for her own child could not be replaced with anything else.

Parwana had given birth to a son, Omar. He had died of cold during a terrible winter. The death had left Saboor and Parwana heart broken. A few months later, Parwana had given birth to Iqbal. Abdullah would watch the love Parwana showered Iqbal with, and he knew that she could never love him and Pari in the same way. They were not her children. They belonged to someone else, and she was gone.

In the wagon, Pari confided in Abdullah her worries about her dog, Shuja. Pari was extremely fond of Shuja, a big dog who walked into the village one day with severed ears and tail. As terrifying as Shuja looked, he never fought back when the village kids threw stones at him or poked him with a stick. He seemed indifferent to all of it, never displaying any sort of emotion.

However, the indifference he displayed with the other kids vanished each time he would see Pari. He loved her unconditionally and displayed an undying loyalty towards her. During the day, he would follow Pari around. At night, he'd wait outside their house until he could be with her again. Now, Pari would be in Kabul for a month, and it worried her that the village boys would try and harm Shuja.

Saboor had informed his children that Nabi, Parwana's brother, had found him a month long job in Kabul. The wealthy people Nabi worked for in Kabul were building a guesthouse in their backyard and needed someone who had experience with construction.

Saboor had taken the job readily. He would never admit it, but Abdullah knew that his father blamed himself for Omar's death. He was unable to provide for his family the way he should have. If he had more work, he would have been able to keep Omar warm, protecting him from the bitter cold that had eventually killed him. Winter was almost upon them again. Abdullah knew that this worried their father.

The children and Saboor had to take a break in their long journey to Kabul and spent the night in the desert. Pari was restless. Sleep wouldn't come to her easily tonight. She pleaded with her father for a story but he gently refused. Something seemed to preoccupy his mind.

Abdullah pulled a blanket over Pari and started the lullaby that he would sing to her every night:

"I found a sad little fairy

Beneath the shade of a paper tree."

Pari sang her verse, already drifting to sleep, "*I know a sad little fairy,*

Who was blown away by the wind one night."

The next day, the two children and their father reached Kabul. Everything the kids knew about Kabul came from the stories they had heard from their Uncle Nabi. As fascinating as those stories were, it hadn't prepared Abdullah and Pari for the chaos and crowd of the big city: the traffic, the teahouses, and restaurants, the bright lights and the noisy streets. For children who had spent their lives in the small village of Shadbagh, this was a new world.

Nabi arrived in a car to pick them up. They watched Kabul from the car window, a city bursting with energy, as their Uncle Nabi drove them to the house where he worked.

They eventually pulled up in front of a magnificent house, two stories high, and surrounded by high walls. The beautiful landscaped garden at the back of the house reminded Abdullah of the *div's* fort. The children observed the house with quiet wonder; it was nothing like anything they had ever seen before.

They were ushered into a large drawing room where they were greeted by Mr. and Mrs. Wahdati. Mr. Wahdati sat on a leather chair and spoke little while Mrs. Wahdati gushed over the children.

Abdullah remembered her from two years ago when their Uncle Nabi had brought her to Shadbagh to meet his family. She had worn a peach, sleeveless dress and dark sunglasses. At their house, she insisted on sitting on the floor with the rest of the family and asked endless questions, as though she were trying to unravel their lives. She was a big city woman trying to pretend she belonged to their small village. Young Abdullah had seen right through the whole charade.

Now, Mrs. Wahdati was offering them cookies, trying to get them to talk. Their father looked down at the floor respectfully, answering any questions directed towards him in few words. Abdullah and Pari stuck to each other, shy and restless, stealing furtive glances at the beautiful Mrs. Wahdati as she talked animatedly, with a cigarette in her mouth.

Later, Mrs. Wahdati insisted on taking the kids to the bazaar. Back in the car, Abdullah sat quietly while Mrs. Wahdati, who seemed to have taken a liking to Pari, listened intently as Pari told her about her dog.

As they drove on, Mrs. Wahdati sighed and looked out of the car, "Kabul is most beautiful at the end of spring.

The way the sun lights up the mountains. The house is usually so quiet; it'll be nice to have a child running around; a little noise, a little life."

Nabi pulled up the car outside a crowded bazaar. The four of them stepped out and joined the hustle and bustle of the bazaar. They stopped by a shoe shop where Mrs. Wahdati picked up a tiny pair of yellow sneakers.

She showed them to Pari, "Would you like these?"

Pari tried them on excitedly as Mrs. Wahdati asked Abdullah to pick a pair of shoes for himself too. The little boy refused. He watched as Pari walked some distance with Uncle Nabi to see how the shoes felt. Tears began forming in his eyes, then poured down his face in earnestness.

"Please don't do it," he begged Mrs. Wahdati. His voice was a small whisper.

She handed him a handkerchief, "You may hate me now, but one day you'll understand. It is for the best."

Weeks passed, and Shadbagh was once again hit by a bitter winter. One morning, Abdullah watched as his father cut down the old oak tree in front of their house. He swung his axe at the tree, over and over again until it was reduced to a stump.

Abdullah sat in front of their house staring at the old windmill in the distance when something caught his eye: a small yellow feather, lying on the ground.

No one had asked about Pari after he and his father returned to their village. It was like she had disappeared from all of their lives. Only Shuja seemed to share Abdullah's sorrow. He would turn up at the house every day, only to be chased away by his father. This didn't seem to stop him, though, and for several days he continued walking up to their door. One morning Abdullah saw him limping towards the hill, head hung low. That was the last time he was ever seen in the village.

Abdullah held onto the yellow feather and began walking toward the windmill. He would never forget Pari screaming out in fear as they tore him away from her. He thought of her beautiful face, her gap toothed smile. It was all gone; vanished, like she had never existed.

He made his way to the back of the windmill and knelt at the base of the tower. He dug through the mud with his bare hands until he felt metal under his fingers. He pulled out the tea tin box and lifted the lid. Her treasured collection was still inside. He placed the yellow feather along with it. '*Maybe, someday,*' he clung on to hope; it was all he could do.

Abdullah knew with certainty now that he would leave Shadbagh the first chance he got. There was nothing left for him in the village except painful memories.

One morning, he would leave his house and walk as far as his feet could take him. He would never return to the village again.

Chapter 3

Spring 1949

Masooma had soiled herself again.

"I'm sorry," she whispered, clearly ashamed.

Parwana forced a weak smile. She had no right to lose patience with her sister. This was her fault. That was a harsh truth she could never hope to escape. She turned Masooma onto her stomach and wiped her clean with a washcloth soaked in water.

It had been four years since their parents had passed away. Masooma had been her responsibility ever since. Between the chores around the house, Parwana would take care of her sister, moving her from time to time, tucking a pillow under her.

During the day, she would sometimes spot Saboor. She would watch him, squatting over the cooking pit outside his small house, his son Abdullah beside him. Her heart would ache every time she caught a glimpse of him, and she would struggle to shift her gaze before he could catch her staring at him.

That night, as Parwana lay down to sleep, Masooma called out to her.

"Can you sleep by me tonight?"

Parwana slipped under the blanket beside her sister.

"You deserve better than me," Masooma whispered, the guilt and shame apparent in her voice.

Parwana's birth was unexpected. Her mother had not known that she was going to have twins. Masooma came out first, and her delivery was easy and quick. Parwana, on the other hand, had caused her mother a lot of pain and agony. They were twins, but the difference between the two sisters had been apparent from the moment of their birth.

Masooma was the easy baby, always eating and sleeping on schedule, and she cried very rarely. Parwana had been the fussy one, requiring round the clock attention. She was always wailing and shrieking, and her antics exhausted her mother. It was colic, and as the sickness passed, Parwana became calmer. Still, for the rest of her childhood, she was destined to live under the shadows of her sister, to be the less liked one between the two of them.

When the sister's were nine years old, they visited Saboor's house for *iftar* to break the fast after Ramadan. While the adults sat together and chatted, the children were left to their own devices.

By this time, Parwana had developed a liking for Saboor. She would steal glances at him, and every time their eyes met, she would blush and look away. Saboor had a unique skill with storytelling, and she would often hear him narrating fascinating stories to the village kids.

Six months ago, Parwana had found the perfect gift for him. She had seen a beautiful notebook with brown leather binding while she was in the bazaar with her mother one day. She knew her mother wouldn't be able to afford to buy it. So, while the shopkeeper was distracted with something else Parwana stealthily slipped the notebook under her sweater. Saboor always talked about wanting to become a writer, and Parwana knew he would love the book she had found for him.

Six months had passed, and the book lay hidden in a corner of her house. Parwana had not found the courage to give the notebook to Saboor. Every night, she promised herself that she would give it to him tomorrow, and every day her courage failed her.

Later that evening, after *iftar* dinner, all the kids rushed outside to play. Parwana sat on a swing tied to the giant oak tree, and Saboor pushed it for her while he narrated a story about the magical powers of the tree. If you knelt before the tree and made a wish, and if the tree agreed to grant it, it would shed exactly ten leaves on your head.

The swing came to a stop and Parwana looked over her shoulder to remind Saboor to keep pushing. She saw Saboor looking at Masooma. He had the notebook - her notebook - in his hands, and they were both smiling at each other. The sight broke her heart.

Later, Masooma explained that she found the book lying around the house and thought it would be the perfect gift for him.

"I hope you don't mind?" she had asked.

Parwana forced a smile and said that she didn't. She spent that night crying quietly while the rest of her family slept.

By the time they were eleven, Masooma had grown into the girl that all the village boys talked about. When the sisters would walk back together from school, they would often encounter a group of boys teasing and heckling. Parwana knew that the noise was for Masooma. They were frightened of her and also in awe of her. Each one of the village boys wanted to be with Masooma. Parwana knew that the teasing flattered her sister, even though she pretended to ignore it. She would often shrug looking at Parwana, "I'm already taken."

At the age of thirteen, the differences in their physical appearance grew more prominent. They were twins, but Parwana, with her pale complexion and flat chest thought of herself as nothing but a pathetic shadow of her beautiful sister. She noticed how Masooma drew attention towards her every time she walked down the road, how the eyes of men followed her every movement, while Parwana walked clumsily beside her.

One morning, when the sisters were seventeen, they were sitting on a branch of the giant oak tree. Masooma couldn't conceal her excitement, "Saboor is going is ask me!" she said.

Parwana pictured her sister's wedding with a sinking heart. Masooma and Saboor were going to be married. Saboor would never know how she felt about him.

Masooma beamed, "Do you want to know how I know this? Let me show you." She let go of the branch with one hand and reached towards her pocket.

In a fit of anger, Parwana pushed down the branch with the heels of her hand, lifting her bottom so that the branch shook. Masooma lost her balance and tumbled forward. The anger passed in an instant, and Parwana watched in panic as her sister fell off the branch. She reached out towards her and grabbed her shirt. The cloth tore, and Masooma fell while her sister looked on in horror. Her lower back slammed into a lower branch, and Parwana heard a sickening crunch before Masooma folded backwards and fell on the ground.

The next few hours were a blur, with every one gathering around her sister, trying to revive her. Among all the chaos, Parwana caught a glimpse of Masooma's closed fist. When someone uncurled her fingers, they found exactly ten crumbled leaves in her palm.

Years had passed since then. It was the spring of 1949, and Parwana had grown to accept that for the rest of her life she would be bound to her sister. She would care for her. This was her punishment, her penance.

Their brother, Nabi, had come for his monthly visits. His hazel eyes, sideburns, and chiseled cheekbones made him a handsome young man. Nabi was working in Kabul and drove to the village in his employer's car every month. Masooma looked forward to these visits. Her brother was her only link to the luxury and glamour of the big city. A year ago, Nabi had taken his sisters to Kabul. He had taken them to the bazaars, cinema, gardens, and restaurants. Masooma was mesmerized. It was the happiest she had been since the accident.

The siblings spent some time in idle chit chat, filling each other in on their lives. Just before he left, Nabi passed some money to Parwana. It was this monthly income from her brother that helped Parwana run the house.

"I was talking to Saboor earlier," Nabi said, "He told me he wanted to marry again. I didn't ask. He pulled me aside and told me."

Nabi watched Parwana as he said this. She looked away, careful not to display any emotion. Nabi understood Parwana in a way that her twin sister didn't. He always suspected that she had harbored feelings for Saboor.

Saboor needed a woman who was not held down by responsibilities, who could devote time to his children. Parwana had a sister to take care of. She couldn't be someone's wife. She had come to accept this long ago.

"I'm sure he'll find someone," Parwana said, trying to feign indifference.

Nabi drove away, and Parwana returned to the house. Masooma was still awake, so she carried her outside and prepared the hookah bowl.

It was a quiet night, and the sisters spent some minutes in silence, taking deep puffs from the hose.

"I want to visit Kabul again," Masooma said.

Parwana looked at her in surprise, then shook her head, "It's a long walk. In your condition, it'll be difficult."

"I spoke to Mullah Shekib when he was visiting this morning. I told him I wished to go to Kabul, and he gave me his mule. I'm bored, Parwana. Please, let's go," Masooma let out a sigh.

They spent the next two days walking through an endless expanse of deserts and mountains, making their way to Kabul. Masooma rode on the mule, Parwana walked beside her. They stopped for the night and Masooma asked her to leave, to go back to Shadbagh.

"You have to do it now. If you hesitate, you'll never be able to do it," Masooma said.

Parwana looked at her in shock, "What about Kabul?" It was all she could get herself to say.

Masooma smiled, "Kabul was never the plan. Don't you understand?"

"No, I won't leave you."

"You're not leaving me. I'm letting you go. This is not the kind of life I want for myself. And it's certainly not the kind of life I want for you," Masooma was crying, "You deserve to be happy. I want you to marry Saboor."

For a moment, Parwana thought of telling her the truth that she had kept from her all these years. It had been her fault. She had caused the accident. She had taken away all the happiness from her sister's life. Parwana stopped herself. Telling the truth would not change anything, except to inflict more pain on her sister.

"I want to smoke now," Masooma said.

Parwana fetched the hookah from the bag and prepared the mixture in the bowl.

"Put in more. A lot more," Masooma said.

Parwana lit a fire and handed the hookah to her sister.

"If you ever loved me, you'll leave now. No goodbyes. Just leave."

Parwana couldn't imagine a life without Masooma. As difficult as it had been, it was the only life she had ever known.

With heart wrenching agony, Parwana forced herself to stand up and turn around. She began walking with the mule by her side. The fire would die soon, and Masooma would be cold. Parwana wanted to run back to her sister, but she knew that if she did, she could never leave again. No one would know, she told herself. It would remain a secret, one that she shared with the mountains only. And she had lived with secrets all her life.

Parwana stood in the dark for a long time, thinking back to their childhood. She was never loved, she was never happy. Everyone had loved Masooma.

Parwana made her decision and began walking again, never turning back. She walked tirelessly throughout the night, the darkness surrounding her like a mother's womb. When the first rays of light lit up the sky, Parwana looked up at the rising sun. It felt like being born. This was her second chance at life.

Chapter 4

Mr. Markos, when I gave you this letter I requested that you not open it until after my death. You're reading this now, which means that I would be gone. I've known you for the past seven years, and I treasure our friendship. I've had the pleasure to have met, through you, a lot of wonderful people- especially Ms. Amra Ademovic and her lovely daughter Roshi.

This letter will be long, with a lot of details. This is because I intend for you to pass this letter on to someone else. The details are for this other person's benefit.

I wonder where I should begin. There is so much to say. Maybe I should begin with the person because of whom I write this letter today, Nila Wahdati.

It was 1949, the year she married Mr. Suleiman Wahdati, that I met her. I had left my village, Shadbagh, and had been working for Mr. Wahdati as cook and driver for two years. Back in my village, I had left behind my two sisters; one of them was an invalid. It shames me sometimes to admit that I left my village in order to escape my responsibilities.

When I started working for Mr. Wahdati, I began living at his residence as well. The house used to be magnificent then, nothing like the state that you found it in when you came to Kabul in 2002. The walls were painted in pure white that sparkled in the sun. In the place where you now hang your friend's picture, there used to be a large circular mirror with a walnut frame.

The foyer was spotted with ceramic vases and a red Turcoman carpet covered a part of the living room floor. The stone tiled kitchen had every appliance you could think of. And the little square holes that you see in your bathroom upstairs? They were once filled with lapis. The garden is overgrown and unkempt now, but during those times, it was the most beautiful place, full of lush greenery. Flower beds and cherry trees dotted the whole area.

I had moved into a small shack at the back of the house. As a young man, the place met all my requirements and suited me fine. I began with cooking for Mr. Wahdati, and when I had proved myself as a good driver, I became his chauffer as well. I believe I had always been a good servant. I familiarized myself with all of Mr. Wahdati's habits and quirks. For instance, he liked to go for a walk every morning, but he didn't like doing this alone. I was expected to accompany Mr. Wahdati on these walks. We hardly talked though, and I always walked behind him.

He was a generous man, and once a month he would let me borrow his car and drive to my village, Shadbagh. The car would catch a lot of attention in the village, and a crowd would gather: children and adults wanting to catch a glimpse of the car.

I would visit my sister, Parwana, and her husband, Saboor. I developed a special fondness for Saboor's children, Abdullah and Pari. They had lost their mother; Parwana was their step-mother. I would offer to take Abdullah for rides in my car, and he always brought along his baby sister. She would sit on his lap as we drove around Shadbagh.

One day, Mr. Wahdati asked me to drive him to a wealthy neighborhood in the city. He was wearing a pin-striped suit, one that I had never seen before. We pulled up in front of a stunning house, bigger than that of Mr. Wahdati's. I waited in the car while Mr. Wahdati made his way inside the house.

Some time passed before Mr. Wahdati emerged from the house again. This time he was accompanied by a beautiful young woman. She wore sunglasses and a short dress that ended just above her knees. At that time, I was in my late twenties.

I admit that in Kabul I had developed the habit of sometimes visiting establishments that met the desires of a young man. Unlike the men in my village who'd wait until marriage to be with a woman, I had laid my eyes on several young women. Still, no one was as beautiful as the lady who accompanied Mr. Wahdati that day. I watched, awe-struck, as she leaned against a wall and smoked a cigarette. There was something poetic about her beauty that left me stunned.

Later that night, Mr. Wahdati confided in me that he was getting married. The news spread like wild fire, and I overheard several distasteful gossips about Mr. Wahdati's bride-to-be. Zahid, the gardener at Mr. Wahdati's house, was especially vocal about the young woman's character. She had been with several men. Worse, she wrote poems about them. I disapproved of the gossip. I was far too loyal to Mr. Wahdati to indulge in such degrading talks.

The wedding took place within a few days of the engagement. It was a small ceremony with a mullah, a witness and the couple. Less than two weeks after I first saw her, Mrs. Wahdati moved into the house. As a servant, I would address her as Bibi Sahib, but for the purpose of this letter, I will dispense of all formality and call her the way I thought of her, as Nila.

Anyone could tell that the marriage was doomed to fail from the beginning. Mr. Wahdati went back to his usual routine of breakfast early in the morning followed by a walk. Nila would sleep late into the mornings, often until noon. I would mechanically go about my chores in the morning, aching to catch a glimpse of her. When she finally walked out of the room, my eyes would follow her, and I would silently observe everything she did.

On most days, Mr. Wahdati spent his time reading or sketching in his study while Nila would write, either in the living room or the veranda. They would hardly spend any time together. Sometimes I would drive Nila when she had to buy something, cigarettes, pens, a notepad, or makeup. On these days, I would make an effort to look more presentable.

While I drove her, I would look for small detours that would prolong the trip by a couple of minutes. Every moment I spent in her presence was important to me. On most days, she hardly spoke to me during these drives.

Then one day, she asked me about my village. It was our first real conversation. After struggling for a few minutes, I managed to think of some interesting things to tell her about my village. Our conversation was punctuated with her laughter. The sound of her laughter echoed through the car and mesmerized me.

I was spellbound by her beauty. Every little movement of hers was so graceful, it left me stunned. Nila did not conform to the notions that most people had about how a woman should behave. She made her own rules. Though most men would disapprove of her character, for me, it only added to her mystery.

Our conversations soon started taking place on a daily basis. I would look forward to them. When she sat sipping coffee on the veranda, I would pretend to busy myself with some task in her vicinity. It gave me a chance to have a conversation with her, and I felt honored that she chose me to punctuate her loneliness.

I learned some things about her life and her family through these conversations. She would tell me about her father. Her mother left for France before the Second World War. She also told me about the year she spent in India with her father when she was very sick.

As she grew more comfortable, she would confide in me complaints about Mr. Wahdati. She would call him aloof and arrogant. Though I tried to defend him, I knew there was some truth in her complaints. There were several instances when Mr. Wahdati would not so much as acknowledge my presence. Still, he had always been generous with me, and for this I was grateful.

Nila never got along with Mr. Wahdati's mother. Whenever I had to drive her and Mr. Wahdati to visit his mother, she would seem annoyed and irritated. It was apparent that Mr. Wahdati's mother did not approve of her.

One day, in the fall of 1950, Nila asked me to take her to my village. Her reason was that I had been serving her for years and she knew nothing about me. Though ashamed to show her my poverty, I was flattered by the interest Nila showed in me, so I agreed to take her to Shadbagh.

I drove her to my village one day. She was wearing high heels and a sleeveless dress. During the drive, she asked me questions about my sister and her family.

When we reached the village, there was the usual crowd of people who gathered around to see the car. An unusual silence spread through the people when Nila stepped out of the car. The adults stared at her, the bare arms and legs creating ripples of murmurs around us. This did not seem to bother Nila as she knelt down and smiled at all the village children, shaking each of their hands.

She insisted on taking off her shoes outside Saboor's house and sat on the floor even though she was offered a chair. I knew that her flawless beauty embarrassed Parwana, who sat quietly in a corner. Abdullah served us tea as Nila tried striking a conversation with Saboor and Parwana. Their little daughter, Pari, was nowhere to be seen, and Nila inquired about her.

"She's asleep in the next room," Abdullah said. He did not seem to approve of Nila.

On Saboor's insistence, Abdullah woke up his sister and carried her to Nila while she was still groggy. I always knew that the bond he shared with his sister was an extraordinary one. Abdullah was more father than sibling to Pari. He doted on her and had taken up her responsibility since the time she was an infant.

Nila was enchanted with Pari, "She's as beautiful as her name, Pari. She indeed looks like a little fairy."

On the drive back to Kabul, Nila seemed lost in thought.

"Your sister has beautiful children," she told me.

I mustered up the courage to say something that I wouldn't otherwise have told her, "By God's Grace, you'll soon have your own."

Sadness crept over Nila's countenance, "You don't understand. That won't happen. They took it all out of me in India. I can never have children."

I longed to comfort her, but I had my boundaries.

For several days after that, Nila remained holed up inside her bedroom. Finally, her father came to visit her one day. The visit seemed to comfort Nila a little, and she slowly got back to her usual routine.

A few days later, Nila told me that she was going to throw a party. The parties had become a frequent occurrence since she had moved into the house. Alcohol was the chief requirement of these parties, and Nila would instruct me on the meals that had to be prepared.

A kind of music that Nila called jazz would play in the background while the guests smoked and drank and laughed freely. Towards the end of the party, Nila would always recite one of her poems. I knew that her poems embarrassed Mr. Wahdati, and he would excuse himself just before these recitals. However, these were always my favorite part of the evening, and I would listen to the poem in rapt attention.

Nila's poems defied tradition. They didn't follow a rhyming pattern or preset meter and they talked about physical love. She wrote about lovers, and as her smoky voice filled the room, I would stand in a corner, enraptured.

A few days after the party, I was serving Mr. Wahdati and Nila lunch when she announced that she needed to buy a new purse. Later, as I was driving her to the market, Nila told me she had to pick up a friend and gave me new directions. We pulled up outside a two storey house and Nila stepped out of the car and entered the house. I had to wait for two hours before she returned. As she climbed into the car, I smelled a second scent, different from the perfume I usually smelt on Nila.

She looked at me from the backseat as she applied a fresh coat of lipstick, “I visited two stores and didn’t find a purse that I liked.” She locked eyes with me in the mirror and waited, willing me into keeping her secret.

Over the next few days, an idea began forming in my mind. I don’t know when I actually thought of it, but once I did, I couldn’t get it out of my head.

Mr. Markos, I honestly believed that my proposal, though painful in the short term, would lead to a greater good in the long term. I admit that I also had a selfish motive, as I could give Nila something that no other man could.

I proceeded to bring my idea to life by first speaking to Saboor. I knew Saboor would never accept money from me, though he was struggling. He was proud, like most Afghani's. He believed in taking care of his family by himself. The decision must have been a heart wrenching one for Saboor.

When I told Nila, her eyes welled up with tears. She took both my hands in her own and looked at me with gratitude, may be even love. I asked her to present the idea to Mr. Wahdati as her own, not mine. I knew he would resist initially, but Mr. Wahdati eventually gave in to Nila's pleas.

I offered Saboor to drive him and Pari to Kabul by car, but he refused. He carried Pari all the way in a wagon. The journey took two days. Maybe it was his way of penance. Maybe he was desperately trying to extend the little time he had with Pari.

Saboor came to Kabul with Pari and her doting brother, Abdullah. The scene that unfolded as the two siblings were separated from one another is something that always weighs heavily on my heart. I had witnessed the pure love these innocent children shared, and that day, I tore them apart. Pari shrieked and cried for her brother. Abdullah struggled, being pulled away by his father. I will never forget that. Every time I think of that day, it breaks my heart.

Pari was only four years old then. Eventually she would forget. She was taught to address me as Nabi instead of Kaka Nabi. Nila was to be called "Maman" and Mr. Wahdati as "Papa." Pari was corrected over and over again until she came to believe that the Wahdati's were her family, and I was merely a servant.

Pari soon melted the heart of Mr. Wahdati who took an unexpected liking to her. He would carry her in a stroller for his morning walks and take her for drives in his car.

For the first time, the Wahdati's resembled a proper family. Mr. and Mrs. Wahdati would take their meals together and accompany Pari to the park. They would stay up with her until she had to be tucked into bed. Eventually, the memories of Shadbagh faded from Pari's mind.

I had secretly hoped that bringing Pari into her life would make Nila see me as more than a servant, but that didn't happen. I receded into the background. Nila did not require me anymore to escape her loneliness.

One day, soon after Pari moved to Kabul, I made one of my monthly visits to Shadbagh. Saboor made it very clear that I was no longer welcome in his home. Even though he had agreed to give Pari away, this had created a rift between me and his family. We could never again sit together and make idle chit chat, pretending like nothing had ever happened. That was the end of my monthly visits to my village. I never saw my sister or the rest of her family ever again.

In the spring of 1955, Mr. Wahdati had a stroke. I ran into his room when I heard Nila screaming my name. Mr. Wahdati seemed to be in the middle of a fit, a line of spittle forming at the corner of his moth. Nila's screams brought in Pari too. She was six by then. She ran to her father's side in panic and started crying. I rushed Mr. Wahdati to the hospital while Nila took care of Pari. Two weeks later, he was brought home again.

Mr. Wahdati was no more his original self. Half of his face was paralyzed, as well as his legs and right arm. He only retained some movement in his left arm. He was an invalid, and his care fell wholly on me. Nila tried, but she was incapable of the care and patience that was now required with her husband.

For several weeks after Mr. Wahdati came back home, the house was always full of visitors inquiring after his health. At these times, Nila would retreat into Pari's bedroom and remain there for hours. Mr. Wahdati's mother would be by his bedside most of the time during those days. Nila's behavior made her furious.

Eventually, the visitors stopped coming. Nila found it unbearable to stay in the same house as her invalid husband. Taking care of him took its toll on her, and I would often find her crying in a corner. It didn't surprise me when Nila told me she was leaving for Paris with Pari.

The day they were leaving, I remember Pari wearing her favorite yellow coat. She kept asking me questions about her Papa. Would they see him soon? Would he visit them in Paris?

There was nothing I could say to her. I kissed the back of her hand and hoped she would have a happy life. Nila asked me to not tell anyone where she was going. She also promised to write to me. As she hugged me, she whispered in my ear, "It was you, Nabi; always. Don't you understand that?"

I didn't know what she meant, and she hurriedly stepped inside the car before I could ask her. As I watched them go, I started weeping. I knew in my heart that I would never see them again.

Since work around the house was now limited, I decided to do all the work on my own. With Mr. Wahdati's permission, I fired all the other servants. He told me I could pay myself any salary I liked, but I refused. I didn't need all that money anyway. I didn't have a family to provide for and I lived in Mr. Wahdati's house.

One day, while cleaning out Mr. Wahdati's closet, I came across a large cardboard box. It had been carefully hidden from view by several coats that were draped over it. I pulled out the box and opened it. It was filled with stacks of Mr. Wahdati's old sketchbooks. I lifted one at the top and opened it. I had always been curious about what Mr. Wahdati drew in these books.

The first page I opened sent a wave of shock through me. I flipped the pages, picked up other sketchbooks from the box, and looked through those.

I could feel my heart racing, it all felt like a blur. Every page had the same subject. Me. Leaning on the verandah, leaning by the car, tying my shoelaces, chopping wood, pouring tea, praying, napping; pages and pages of sketches, all with me as the subject.

It was you Nabi; always.

I understood now. I left the room and walked out of the house. I walked for hours, never looking back. How could I go back? After everything I knew? It was impossible. I wasn't disgusted by what I had seen, but it made me uncomfortable. By the end of the evening, I walked back to the house. Only I could take care of Mr. Wahdati. He had no one else.

I decided I would look for someone to take my place. Until then, I would stay. I started looking for someone without informing Mr. Wahdati, but I could never find anyone I could trust with taking care of my employer. So, years passed, and I still remained with Mr. Wahdati.

Our relationship grew into a close friendship of sorts. We were more informal with each other, and I had taken to calling him by his name, Suleiman.

One day, I bought him a wheelchair. It had been years since he had stepped out of the house, and I wanted him to stop spending all his days in his bed.

I insisted that Suleiman use the wheelchair. After that, our old tradition of morning walks began again.

We had a new neighbor around this time, Mr. Bashiri. He and his brother had moved into a house across from us with their wives. Suleiman and I would often come across Mr. Bashiri during our walks, and he became one of the few people we started conversing with.

Years passed. Suleiman's mother passed away. Mr. Bashiri and his brother became fathers to two beautiful boys, Idris and Timur. I was well past forty by this time, though I never knew my real age.

"You should think of getting married," Suleiman told me one day, as we played a game of chess.

I smiled at him. I knew by then that I was never going to get married.

"I remember when I hired you," Suleiman continued, "You were a terrible cook and an even worse driver."

He had never told me this before, "Why would you hire me then?"

"I had never seen anyone as beautiful as you," Suleiman turned his eyes towards me as he said this, "Please don't be angry at me, Nabi. I have to say this to you. I have loved you for a long time now. I loved you ever since I saw you walk into my house the first time, twenty-one years ago."

I didn't know what to say. Words failed me. I could hear the relief in Suleiman's voice, now that he had confessed his feelings for me.

"You should find yourself a wife, Nabi. I'm willing to let you go," he continued.

"Maybe one of these days I will, and then you'll be sorry," I said, grinning at him, trying to wave away his confession with a joke.

By then, I knew that I would never leave Suleiman's side. I did not need to marry. I already had a home where I found comfort and companionship. Isn't that why people marry in the first place? To have someone they can spend their lives with, someone they can call family? I found my family with Suleiman. As for the physical urges I had to be with a woman, Kabul was a big city, and there were several places where I could satisfy these desires.

"If you have decided not to marry, then I would like to ask you something," Suleiman said, "but you must promise me to accept it, whatever it is." I agreed, and Suleiman made his request.

By this time, Afghanistan was engulfed in war. The country was ripped apart by people who bombed, looted, raped, and killed. I was glad for Nila and Pari. Kabul had become hell for women; they would have had a difficult time had they stayed. Several of our neighbors escaped the country while they still had the chance. Most of them looked to settle down in Pakistan or Iran. Mr. Bashiri also left with his family and children. He was moving to the United States.

Kabul tried to stay out of the war as much as it could until it also became a victim in the 1990's. Fighting broke out within the city limits as men carrying Kalashnikovs barged into the city. Suleiman stayed in the house and refused to venture out. It was during this period that the house suffered most of the damages that you, Mr. Markos, witnessed when you occupied it in 2002.

Militiamen would make their way into the house, destroying everything in their way, and taking away anything that caught their fancy. They took away most of the furniture, paintings, rugs, and vases. They even dug out the lapis from the bathroom floor. There was nothing I could do to stop them. The war ended with the arrival of the Taliban. But Afghanistan's sorrow didn't end. If anything, it only became worse.

In the summer of 2000, I walked into Suleiman's room to find him having another stroke. I wanted to call a doctor, but Suleiman stopped me. He pointed to a drawer which I opened. I found an envelope with my name scribbled on it.

"Not yet. It's not yet time," I said

"You promised," Suleiman groaned.

I gave up and slipped into bed next to him. I gently placed a kiss on his cracked lips and held him for a long time, until he finally closed his eyes in peace.

The letter that Suleiman left for me was his will. He had bequeathed to me everything he owned, including the house, but the house made me restless. I couldn't stay there alone, so I moved back into my old shack in the backyard. I took with me the box containing Suleiman's sketches.

I met you in 2002. You had come to Kabul for humanitarian work, to help a broken country. You were looking for a house to rent, and I offered you mine. I refused to take rent from you. You were helping my country, and it was the least I could do for you in return.

You would have parties in the house, and I made the acquaintance of several of your friends. It was my greatest honor to have met Miss Amra Ademovic. She was an exceptional human being. When I told her about Nila, she helped me find out more about her through the internet. Nila had become an accomplished poet. She had died in Paris in 1974.

I know I don't have too much time left, Mr. Markos. I would like to thank you for letting me be your friend, for confiding in me about your life and your family. You'd tell me stories about your mother and friend, Thalia, who live in Greece. I have enjoyed our conversations.

I will take the liberty to ask you for two favors. The first is that you have me buried in the Ashuqan-Arefan cemetery. Find a plot close to Suleiman's grave.

The second is that I beg you to find my niece, Pari, and give her this letter. I have left everything to her in my will. She is, after all, Mr. Wahdati's daughter, the rightful owner of his property.

Tell her that I apologize for any pain I have caused her. I never imagined the endless consequences that my actions would cause. I hope she has found happiness, love, and peace in her life.

Thank you, Mr. Markos. May God bless you.

Your friend always,

Nabi

Chapter 5

Spring 2003

Amra Ademovic was a Bosnian nurse at the Wazir Akbar Khan Hospital in Kabul. She fixed Idris and Timur with a stern gaze, "You can't show any reaction at all. It'll upset her."

They were standing at the end of the men's wing of the hospital. The little girl, Roshi, had only an uncle who visited her. Since the uncle would not be allowed into the women's wing, Roshi had to be placed here, at the end of the hallway of the men's wing.

Amra looked at the men, making sure they understood. They were not supposed to display shock when she pulled back the curtains. As the curtains were drawn away, Idris had to swallow a gasp before it could escape his lips. For Timur, this was harder, "Oh! Oh!" he exclaimed, too shocked to say anything else. Roshi couldn't be any more than nine years old. Fate had been cruel to her.

Amra protectively pulled the curtains around Roshi again. She looked at Timur sternly but her expression was more flirtatious than angry. Idris wasn't surprised. Timur always had this effect on women.

Idris and Timur had returned to Kabul to reclaim their father's property. With real estate prices shooting up in the city, they were sure to make a fortune. Timur, in his usual flair would tell everyone who'd listen that they had come back to their homeland to do what they could for a country that had fallen victim to war. They wanted to "reconnect," to "give back." All words, of course. Idris knew this. Back in California, Timur ran a successful real estate mortgage business. Idris was a doctor. They had lived in the United States for twenty years.

Timur's father had sent the two of them to Kabul to claim their property. Idris' father had died of cancer nine years ago. Timur had stayed by his side during that time. While Idris had mourned his father's death, Timur was the one who greeted visitors who had come to pay respects and made funeral arrangements.

Timur had a unique skill with people. It is what made him a successful businessman and also what attracted women to him. When Idris was in his second year of medical residency, he and his wife, Nahil, were struggling to make ends meet. Again, Idris had only Timur to turn to for money. His cousin lent him money without a moment's hesitation. Timur had always been generous with people.

While Idris was the quiet, unassuming one, Timur liked to make a big show. Even though he always came through during difficult times, Idris disliked the fact that Timur would brag about it to everyone. For instance, everyone in his family knew that Timur had loaned Idris money. It had been humiliating. Still, Idris couldn't hold anything against his cousin. Timur was always there when Idris needed him.

That evening, after their trip to the hospital, the cousins made their way to the neighborhood where they had spent their childhood. They had been invited to a party by Mr. Markos. They stopped in front of a two story house, small by American standards. But in Kabul, this was considered luxury. Like most houses in Kabul, this one had been ruined by war. One could still see faint shadows of its past splendor.

"Do you remember this house?" Timur asked.

"It belonged to Mr. Wahdati," Idris replied.

Mr. Markos greeted the cousins in the foyer. There were several guests sitting on cushions around the room and soft jazz music played in the background.

As they were handed drinks, Idris observed, “I remember this house from my childhood. It is a beautiful house.”

“You can tell that to the owner yourself,” Mr. Markos smiled and pointed towards the thin, old man who was making his way toward them.

“Nabi?” Timur exclaimed.

The man looked confused, “Forgive me. Do I know you?”

Timur and Idris introduced themselves, and Nabi instantly remembered. He warmly embraced both of them.

“You own this place?” Timur asked

“Mr. Wahdati left the house to me in his will,” Nabi explained.

While the cousins were catching up with Nabi, Amra walked into the room. She made her way straight to

Nabi and kissed him on his cheek while putting her arms around him.

“I’m extremely fond of this man,” She announced to the little group.

Nabi laughed shyly.

Markos introduced Amra to his guest, “She is the hardest working woman in Kabul.”

For the next few hours, Timur mingled with the guests. He narrated stories and cracked jokes, and everyone seemed to enjoy his company. Idris, on the other hand, felt lost. Parties made him uncomfortable.

He walked around looking at the posters and photographs that Markos hung around the house. A crude, black and white, blurry photograph caught his attention. It had captured a young girl with black hair. She had her back to the camera. The lower left-hand corner of the photo looked like it had been burned.

Idris eventually retreated to the verandah, carrying a glass of wine with him. A few minutes later, Amra joined him.

"I think your cousin embarrasses you," She observed.

It was true. Idris hated the charade that Timur put on. Each time they walked on the streets of Kabul, Timur struck up conversations with the Afghanis. He pretended he understood their sorrow, shared their pain. He and Timur had led comfortable lives in the United States. They didn't know anything of the tragedy that had befallen Afghanistan. Timur was being a hypocrite.

"We were lucky. We escaped from this place just in time," Idris tried to explain.

"I understand," Amra replied.

The conversation veered towards Roshi. Amra told Idris her story.

Roshi lived with her parents, two sisters, and a baby brother in a small village. There had been an argument over the family property between her father and her uncle, her father's older brother. Last month, the brother had visited their family and made amends with the father. It had been a night of celebration, as the family gathered around to eat together. They talked and laughed most of the evening.

Towards the end of the evening, the uncle excused himself to use the outhouse. When he returned, he was carrying an axe in his hand. He struck Roshi's father from behind, then attacked her mother. Roshi's sisters began screaming and made a run for the hallway.

Her uncle first struck one sister with his axe and then followed the other to the bedroom where Roshi heard muffled screams followed by a deafening silence. Roshi looked around her in panic. There was no way to escape. Her uncle had locked the front door.

In panic, Roshi dragged her younger brother and ran into the yard. She realized too late that the yard was surrounded by high walls. As her uncle made his way towards them, the brother threw himself into the *tandoor*. Roshi could hear him screaming as he was engulfed by flames and then she saw an axe whooshing down on her.

Amra stopped, and Idris remained silent, too shocked to say anything. He thought of Roshi lying in the hospital, her shaved head, and the brain tissue spilling out from a wide crack on her crown.

"No one survived. Roshi has a maternal uncle who visits her sometimes," Amra said, "I fight for her. I'll never stop fighting."

The next day, Idris decided to stay behind while Timur made plans to visit the town of Istalif. After Timur left, Idris made his way to the bazaar. He purchased what he required and carried it with him to the hospital. Idris made his way to Roshi's bed where he found Amra and another man, presumably Roshi's uncle.

Idris handed Roshi a box. He had bought her a small TV and VCR. He was able to find four films that he thought she would like- E.T., Babe, Toy Story, and The Iron Giant. He sat with Roshi on her bed, and they watched one of the movies together.

Idris visited Roshi every day after that. Timur eventually found out.

"It's a good thing you are doing," he had said, "Don't let her get too attached to you though. We are leaving in a week."

Idris knew he was right. Roshi had started addressing him as Kaka Idris. She would look forward to his visits and would get upset if he was late. He had begun to feel responsible for Roshi.

The day before he left Kabul, he inquired with Amra about the operation Roshi needed.

"I can make arrangements to fly her to California. I know some neurosurgeons. I could make it happen," he said to Amra.

"What about the money?"

"We'll find the funding. If nothing works, I'll pay for it myself."

"Thank you," Amra smiled at him with gratitude. She was beaming and tears sprung to her eyes.

Idris' wife, Nahil, and his sons, Lemar and Zabi, picked him up from the airport.

Nahil questioned Idris about Kabul. She asked him about the restaurants and his accommodation. Insignificant questions for Idris who had seen for himself the tragedy in Kabul. His sons played in the backseat, uninterested in his stories of Kabul.

Idris longed for Afghan food, so the family made their way to Abe's Kabob House. It was a small restaurant that Idris and his family visited often. It was run by one of Idris' patients, Abdullah and his wife Sultana.

Idris was well acquainted with Abdullah. He was married in Pakistan in the 1970s. In 1982, they were granted asylum in the US. It was the same year that their daughter, Pari, was born.

On returning home, Idris found that his house was in disarray. He panicked for an instant before remembering that they were in the middle of remodeling the house. Nahil informed him that the home theatre would be set up within the week.

A home theatre; it felt like such a silly idea to him now. A few nights later, Idris confided his guilt to Nahil, "It feels like we have too much. All this stuff; it's unnecessary."

She looked at him thoughtfully, "I think you're struggling with survivor's guilt."

"It's just that - I want to do something about what I saw in Kabul."

"Do it then. You don't have to feel guilty about what we have; we've worked hard for it. If you want to make a difference to the lives in Afghanistan, then go ahead and do that. Put your guilt to use."

Nahil was right. He knew that she provided for a Columbian kid named Miguel. It was time he gave back to society too.

Later, while checking his mail, Idris found an email from Amra inquiring whether he had spoken to a neurosurgeon yet.

Along with the mail was a letter from Roshi.

Salaam, Kaka Idris,

I hope you've arrived safely in America. I miss you and watch the films you got me every day. I feel sad that you're not here to watch it with me. I'm feeling better now. Amra takes good care of me. I hope to see you soon in California. Please say salaam to your family from me.

With my respects,

Roshi

Idris sent back a letter telling Amra that he would talk to his boss this week. He sent back a small note to Roshi telling her that he missed her too.

The next day was a Monday. It was Idris' first day at work after returning back from Kabul. He found that his schedule was packed for the entire day, patients to see, meetings to attend, and hundreds of emails to answer. He struggled to get through the week.

During this time, he received two more letters from Amra, and he kept postponing his reply. Finally, overwhelmed with guilt, he wrote back to her saying that he was trying his best.

The next week, Idris had a meeting with his chief, Joan Schaeffer. He informed her about Roshi and her condition.

"I don't know if the board will approve of flying the girl down here. She would require several complicated procedures to cure her injuries. A lot of legal issues will be involved," Joan said.

"I understand," Idris replied. There was nothing he could do.

"You could find a humanitarian group that could help you…"

Idris cut her short, "I'll look into it. Thank you."

The days passed in a blur. Idris' house was remodeled and his home theatre set up. Roshi and Kabul faded into the background. He no longer felt the same powerful urge to help her as he had before. He had come to accept that there was nothing he could do. He had tried. He ignored every letter that he received from Amra after that.

Six years passed. One day, Idris found himself standing in a line in a bookstore. He had a book in his hand, as did everyone else in the line. They all wanted to get it signed. It was a great story; the story of a survivor.

Idris had not read the book. He doubted he ever would. He didn't even want to get it signed. He just wanted to see her again.

He opened the book, flipping past the bio of the co-author, the one who had done the actual writing.

He stopped at the page with Roshi's picture. There was no sign of her injury, no scar that could be noticed.

Idris read the dedication:

To the two angels in my life: my mother, Amra, and my Kaka Timur. You are my saviors. I owe you everything.

Guilt and shame washed over Idris.

The line moved, and he was standing in front. His heart raced as he watched Roshi look up at him. No sign of recognition passed over her face as she took his book and scribbled in it. Idris was speechless; he suddenly had nothing to say. The salesclerk asked him to move along, there were people waiting behind him. Idris looked down at what Roshi had scribbled in his book. Words failed him. He looked at Roshi helplessly before the salesclerk moved him away from her table.

In his car, Idris opened the book again with trembling hands.

There was no signature. Instead Roshi had written two short sentences:

Don't worry. You're not in it.

The words hurt him. He would have preferred if Roshi had looked at him with contempt or said something curt. These words felt like an act of charity. It made him feel like a coward.

Idris left the book at a bench nearby. He sat in his car for a while, hands shaking, head spinning. It took him sometime to compose himself and drive away.

Chapter 6

February 1974

Parallaxe (Winter 1974)

Editor's Note

Dear Readers,

For five years, we have published quarterly issues with each issue featuring a little-known poet. This has become a popular and cherished tradition at Parallaxe. Our staff and readers have always looked forward to these features.

However, this issue is particularly special to us. Nila Wahdati, a talented Afghan poet, was interviewed by us shortly before her untimely death. This was her last interview. We share the sadness of her loss with the literary community.

Nila Wahdati is survived by her daughter.

Pari and Julien were just about to enter the elevator when the phone started ringing from inside Julien's apartment, and Pari knew who she would find on the line.

"We're late, Pari. We should leave," Julien was insistent, but Pari's conscience was weighing on her. She had to get the phone.

"It could be important," Pari said, and went into the apartment. It was a small flat, and Pari was quick to reach the phone.

Pari heard a man's voice. He was asking for Madame Nila Wahdati's daughter.

"She is my mother," Pari replied, "What happened?"

The man introduced himself as Dr. Delauny. Her mother had an accident. Pari closed her eyes. She wasn't surprised, but she was tired. This was not the first time she had been called by a hospital. She stood by the phone recalling all of her hospital visits, injuries on the head, stitches, tetanus injections, antibiotics, dressings, the list was endless.

She had to check on Maman in the hospital. This annoyed Julien. They had lunch plans with some friends, but Pari had to go.

Excerpt from 'Afghan Songbird'

Interview with Nila Wahdati by Etienne Boustouler

Parallaxe 84 (Winter 1974)

I'm sitting with Nila Wahdati, age forty-four, in her small thirteenth floor apartment. She wears a bandana over her brow and a purple blouse with jeans. She is smoking a cigarette and drinking Chardonnay, though it's only eleven in the morning.

EB: Tell me about your parents?

NW: My mother was French; Parisian. My father was born into a royal family in Afghanistan. They met in 1927, at a formal dinner in the Royal Palace.

EB: I gather you moved to France in 1955. The country did not suit you?

NW: I moved to protect my daughter. There was nothing I could offer her except a life of repression in Afghanistan. It was pathetic, and I had to make sure she wouldn't be trapped in a life like that.

EB: Your daughter must be grateful to you for that?

Nila lights a cigarette

NW: Sadly, children are not always what you expect them to be.

Pari made her way to the emergency room and found Dr. Delaunay. He informed her that her mother was drunk when she was brought to the hospital, "The nurses in the hospital seemed to know how to handle her, though. I understand she's been here several times before. I'm new here," he said.

Pari was shown a corner of the emergency room and she walked toward her mother's bed. Her mother was wearing the hospital gown the wrong way, her caesarian scar clearly visible. It was a vertical scar and it had always puzzled Pari. Caesarian scars were usually horizontal. When Pari had asked her mother about it once, she said that the doctors had given her some medical reasons that she no longer remembered.

Pari sat by Nila's bedside as she slept and thought back to the fateful day when she had first come across Julien. It was ten years ago in 1963, in an emergency room similar to the one she was sitting in. Pari was fourteen, and she had sprained her ankle.

Julien was also a patient at the hospital, and he had struck up a conversation with her mother. He politely asked about her daughter, "Pari, like Paris without the 's.' It means 'fairy' in Farsi," Nila had told him.

A few days later, Pari and her mother met Julien for dinner. He was a professor of economics at the Sorborne. Nila and Julien had spent the evening flirting with each other and talking about their interests. Pari spent most of the evening trying hard not to stare at Julien. She was enamored by his charm and intellect. Pari observed her mother, as she giggled flirtatiously, always playing with her hair. Nila made for a beautiful sight.

Pari often felt detached from her. She knew she wasn't anything like her mother. There was nothing about her appearance that suggested she was her mother's daughter. Pari didn't think she bared any resemblance with her father either.

She had a few pictures of him from her childhood home in Kabul. Seeing her father's photographs always brought back faint memories, memories that Pari could never piece together. All her life, she had felt like something was amiss. She could never figure out what it was, but some absence echoed through her life and followed her wherever she went.

She had once asked her mother about it.

"Obviously, it's because you miss your father. You never got the chance to know him," she had said, but Pari had always felt like there was something else, something more.

Pari saw Julien several times over the next few weeks. One morning, as she carried a cup of coffee to her mother's room, she found Julien sitting on the edge of the bed, putting on his wristwatch. Pari stopped in surprise, but she couldn't turn away. She was hopelessly attracted to

Julien. He had looked up, sensing her presence, and had smiled at her.

The only person Pari confided her feelings in was her friend, Collette. Collette always theorized that Julien was only with her mother so that he could eventually get to Pari. Pari had a feeling she was right. Julien remained with her mother for six months after which they parted ways. Pari would not see him again for many years.

Excerpt from 'Afghan Songbird'

An Interview with Nila Wahdati by Etienne Boustouler

Parallaxe 84 (Winter 1974)

I look around the apartment, and the photograph of a little girl in a bright yellow jacket catches my eye. I ask about the picture

NW: My daughter, Pari. It means 'fairy' in Farsi.

EB: Tell me more about your daughter.

NW: She studies mathematics in the Sorbonne. I don't know where she gets the ability to study that subject.

EB: Maybe it's her way of rebelling. You've been quite a rebel, too.

She laughs

NW: Rebel for what? I have given her all the freedom she could ever wish for. There is nothing she lacks in her life. She's living with an older man, now. What I think about him will never matter. In France, children don't live by their parents rules.

I ask her to tell me more about her early life. She excuses herself from the room and when she returns, she's carrying a black and white photograph of a stern-looking man.

NW: My father. The photograph is from 1929, the year I was born. He was a handsome young prince with a beautiful French wife. However, their relationship was a strained one. I never saw them display any sort of affection towards each other. For most of their marriage, they slept in different rooms. He

made sure he spent a few minutes with me every day. He tried hard to be an affectionate father, but it never came naturally to him. Most days he would tire of me fairly quickly.

Later that day, Nila was discharged from the hospital, and Pari accompanied her to her apartment.

"I have an interview coming up for a poetry magazine," Nila informed her.

As Pari entered her mother's apartment, she found the whole house in disarray. Everything lay scattered, and in a corner lay a piece of cloth soaked in blood. Pari sat by her mother's bed until she fell asleep. She spent the rest of the night tidying up the house. As she scrubbed the floors and washed the vessels, Pari thought back to the day she met Julien again. It was a year ago, in 1973; she had seen him for the first time in almost ten years.

Pari had been sharing a flat with Collette, who at that time had taken to protesting against animal cruelty. She had arranged a march outside the Canadian Embassy against the hunting of seals and had insisted that Pari join in the event. The march turned out to be a failure as only thirty people turned up for it. Pari watched Collette yelling at a young man named Eric, who she had learned was responsible for getting people to participate in the march.

Someone tapped her on her shoulder, "You look like you need rescuing."

Pari turned around and was shocked to see Julien. His hair was longer, and he had aged a little, but he still looked as attractive and charming as he did ten years ago, if not more so.

The two of them spent the rest of the evening catching up with each other in a small café.

"You've grown into a beautiful young woman, Pari," he told her, and she dismissed his complement.

He talked about his travels to Jordan and Iraq, while Pari confided in him her wish to go to Afghanistan. She and Collette had decided to go together.

"I want to visit my childhood home, travel my country. I vaguely remember we had a servant, who was very much like family to us. His name was Nabi," she told him.

Out of politeness, Julien asked about Nila. Pari told him about her declining bookstore business, but they didn't talk about her much.

Pari moved in with Julien a few weeks later. She knew that she had to inform her mother. It was important to her that Nila knew about her relationship. When Pari called her the next day, her mother had already heard the news. She had found out from Collette.

"Are you angry?" Pari asked

"It wouldn't matter to you, would it?"

Pari sighed, "I don't want to hurt you, Maman."

Nila laughed; a piercing, ugly laughter, "You are nothing like me," she had said, "but I suppose that is expected. I don't know what kind of person you are in your blood. You're a stranger to me."

Pari didn't understand her mother's words, and Nila didn't care to explain.

Excerpt from 'Afghan Songbird'

An Interview with Nila Wahdati by Etienne Boustouler

Parallaxe 84 (Winter 1974)

EB: I understand that your parents separated when you were a child?

NW: Yes, they divorced in 1939. I was ten years old. My mother left for France, but she couldn't take me along with her. She died of pneumonia during World War 2. I was devastated. I always planned to live with her in France after the war.

EB: How did you get along with your father?

NW: We had our problems. I was young, bold, and adventurous. He didn't approve of most of the things I did. Then there were the men,- most of them the wrong sort. News of my rendezvous would reach my father; people on the streets began gossiping about me. In a fit of anger, he would beat me. I took to writing scandalous, passionate poems.

Nila Wahdati's poems from this period are probably some of her best. They are insightful and mesmerizing poems about loneliness and sorrow, the tragedy of separation, the heart ache that comes along

with young love. They spoke of repression and a desire to be free.

EB: These poems, you don't follow a rhythm or meter that I understand is fundamental to Farsi poetry. You spoke in detail about things that were insignificant, mundane. This was fairly groundbreaking and maybe if you were living in a less repressive country, it would have made you some sort of a pioneer.

NW: Imagine that.

She smiles; a bitter smile.

NW: I can tell you that no one was touting me in Kabul. My character was questioned on the streets and by my father. He disapproved of my poems; said that I would be dragging the family name through the mud. I did not care for my father's version of morality and respect. I only wanted to be free. The poems were my way of breaking free.

EB: What happened next?

NW: I fell critically ill when I was nineteen. My father took me to Delhi for treatment. Everything

changed after I came back. My close brush with death made me feel diminished, insignificant. For a long time I suffered with depression. The next year, I married Suleiman Wahdati. My husband was a decent man, but our marriage was doomed to fail. He was in love with our chauffer. He died of a stroke when our daughter was six. Soon after, I moved to France. I did it for my daughter, but she has never appreciated the sacrifices I made for her.

EB: Are you disappointed by your daughter?

NW: I've come to believe she is my punishment.

A year after her mother's funeral, Pari came home to find a package on her bed. It was from Julien. She had broken up with him nine months ago.

You should update your forwarding address. This was sent to Nila and then forwarded to my address. Read it at your own peril.

Pari flipped through the pages of the magazine. There was more about her life within these pages than her mother had ever told her. Nila had never spoken to Pari about her father. Was it true that he loved Nabi?

Perhaps this was her mother's intention; to turn Pari's world upside down before killing herself. She had to go to Afghanistan. She needed to find answers.

A few days later Pari met Collette, who brought along with her a young man, Eric Lacombe. Pari recognized him from the seal hunting protest she had attended months ago. He was the boy Collette had been yelling at.

Collette got along with Eric for Pari's benefit. She thought he would be a good match for her, and she was right. Pari and Eric got married in 1977.

Soon after, they made plans to go to Afghanistan. Their plans came to a standstill when Pari discovered that she was pregnant. They needed the money; they had to buy a bigger apartment. Making a trip would be reckless and irresponsible. Pari gave birth to Isabelle. In 1981, her son, Alain, was born, and two years later, she gave birth to Thierry.

Pari's career began looking up when she was hired as a professor at a prominent university. Eric became a successful playwright.

Pari often wondered what sort of grandmother Nila would have made. As strenuous as their relationship was, Pari missed having her mother around.

Her husband and children provided her with everything she could ever wish for. The emptiness that she had felt for most of her life faded, and Pari no longer felt the need to visit Afghanistan. She had a happy marriage and a loving family.

It all ended in 1944, when Eric died of a heart attack. At the age of forty-eight, Pari was a widow.

By 2010, her children had grown up and moved away. Isabelle lived with her husband, a few blocks away from Pari's apartment. She would visit her often. Alain lived in Madrid while Thierry travelled the world on humanitarian work.

Pari had grown old and week. She suffered from swan neck deformity, which left her hands ugly and twisted. One day, she waited by her phone for a call she was expecting from a man who contacted her through Facebook with something important to say.

Marcos Varvaris called at 9:30 am. Pari listened to him patiently as he told her the political scenario in Kabul, before finally confiding to her the reason for his call. He lived in the house that used to belong to her parents. The last owner, Nabi, passed away and left a letter for her.

"Could you read me the letter?" Pari asked with her heart racing. She had known for a long time that her mother had lied to her about her childhood. Now, Pari was on the verge of finding out the truth.

Markos patiently read out the letter. By the end of it, Pari's hands were trembling. From the depths of her mind, memories begin to surface in flashes: a red wagon rolling through a desert, a dog, a giant tree, and most distinctly of all, a tiny hand holding hers. Pari looked for the face, but it evaded her. A verse from a Farsi song suddenly came to her:

"I know a sad little fairy,

Who was blown away by the wind one night."

It was about time she made her trip to Kabul.

Chapter 7

Summer 2009

Adel was watching his father, his Baba Jan, make a passionate speech to the crowd. He was addressing the locals from the small town of Shadbagh-e-Nau, "New Shadbagh."

The crowd looked on in admiration and respect as he talked about reviving war-torn Afghanistan. He was flanked by two Klanishkov bearing bodyguards.

At the end of his speech, the crowd burst into applause. The villagers approached Baba Jan later, some to pay respects, some to offer prayers, and some to make requests. Baba Jan personally attended to each one. He would lean in and listen to them carefully.

Adel had heard several stories about Baba Jan's jihad days, stories of courage and sacrifice. He had been injured several times during war, but he had survived. Now, he worked in building up Afghanistan from scratch. He had recently built a new girl's school in Shadbagh-e-Nau.

Just as they were approaching their car, Adel spotted an old man with a grey beard and spectacles making his way towards them. A boy in rag tag clothes, the same age as Adel, followed him.

Kabir, Baba Jan's bodyguard, stopped him from getting too close to the car.

"I just want to talk to the commander," the old man said. Baba Jan guided Adel into the backseat of their Land Cruiser and stepped in after him. The car drove away, before the old man could say anything else.

They were living in Shadbagh-e-Kohna, Old Shadbagh. The village was now deserted; except for the enormous house that Adel lived in with his parents. The house was three stories high, with nine bedrooms and seven bathrooms. The house got lonely at times, especially when his father was not around.

Baba Jan was leaving to oversee his cotton factory in Helmand. He would be gone for two weeks. This upset Adel.

Later that day, Adel watched a scene unfolding in the foyer. The doorbell rang and Kabir answered the door. It was the old man again, wanting to speak to Baba Jan.

"He's left for business. He'll be gone for three months," Kabir told him.

"That's not what I heard. I am going to wait for him."

"You can't wait here," Kabir said

"I'll wait by the road," the old man backed away from the door, the boy following him.

Adel had been living in Shadbagh for two years. He didn't have a single friend here. He was homeschooled and could never step out of the perimeter of their compound without a bodyguard. He knew that his mother, Aria, also felt terribly lonely. The silence and emptiness of the house would frustrate both of them. On the days when Baba Jan wasn't around, Adel and his mother would try to be each other's reprieve.

Adel would spend a lot of his time walking around the compound. Here, there was a tree stump of what looked like a giant oak tree. He had once counted the rings on it with Baba Jan; the tree had been incredibly old. Whoever cut it down was a fool, Baba Jan had said.

A few days after his father left, Adel couldn't stay at home any longer. He knew the timings of the guard at the gates and managed to sneak out when they were not around.

Walking down the road, Adel spotted a boy squatting under the shade of a brick shed. It was the same boy who Adel had seen with the old man. He knew he was meant to keep a distance from people he didn't know, but Adel longed for company. It had been ages since he had spoken to someone his own age.

The boy introduced himself as Gholam. They were soon discussing soccer. Adel challenged him to a best of five games which Gholam lost miserably. They played another set which he lost again.

Adel learned that this was Gholam's first visit to Afghanistan, though his parents had lived in the country before. He was born in a refugee camp in Pakistan. He spent all his life there with his mother, his father, Iqbal and his grandmother, Parwana. Recently the camp shut down, and they were ordered to leave. Gholam and his family were living in a tent, in the open field with the windmill. "This place is my father's home. He wants us to settle here again," Gholam said.

Before he could leave, Adel asked Gholam for another rematch. Gholam replied that this time he would be playing for the Zidane jersey that Adel was wearing.

The game ended with Gholam saving all of Adel's shots. Adel handed him the jersey and was surprised when tears sprang to his eyes. He felt embarrassed.

Every day, for the rest of the week, Adel would sneak out of his house to meet Gholam. One day, Gholam handed Adel his jersey. He confessed that he had sold the jersey to a village boy to buy new shoes. Later, he had bullied the boy into returning the jersey to him.

Adel found Gholam interesting and mysterious. His fascinating stories and cryptic remarks often made Adel wonder if he had understood what Gholam was saying.

One day, Gholam told Adel about his grandmother. She would narrate to him a story that her husband, his grandfather, loved telling people. It was the story about a tree that granted wishes. One had to kneel before the tree and make a wish. If the tree agreed to the wish, it would shed exactly ten leaves on the person's head. His grandfather, Saboor, cut down the tree years ago, when his father was still a kid.

Adel listened attentively to the story. Silence followed as Adel began putting the pieces together.

"Wait. Your grandfather cut down our tree?"

"Your tree? It wasn't your tree," for the first time Adel heard contempt in Gholam's voice, "My family had a house here. Your father destroyed people's homes to build that monstrosity that you call a house. You cried when I took your jersey, I know you did. Imagine my family coming all the way from Pakistan just to find that their property had been stolen from us."

"My father is not a thief!" Adel yelled.

"My father has the ownership documents for the property. He is going to go to court with it. I'm going to prove you wrong," Gholam spat, "And one more thing. Ask your father why he keeps going to Helmand. I assure you it's not cotton."

Gholam's words echoed through Adel's mind over and over again for the next few days. His father had often told him that the world was a hard place for the poor and they shouldn't be blamed for their anger.

Three days later, Adel met Gholam again.

"I went with my father to the courthouse yesterday. The judge told us that our ownership documents were destroyed in a fire. Gone, just like that, how convenient for your father," Gholum turned around and walked away.

That evening, Adel's father returned to the house and a party was thrown. Sometime during dinner the guests heard a loud noise, someone had thrown a rock through the window.

The women screamed in fear as Baba Jan and his bodyguards ran towards the door. Adel followed them. It was the old man. He was standing on the front steps with a rock in each hand. Adel's mother dragged him upstairs as Baba Jan and his bodyguards circled the man.

In his room, Adel wept uncontrollably. He didn't want to believe it, but he was afraid he knew what was going to happen to Gholam's father.

Days passed. No one had spoken about the incident since that night. Adel suddenly realized how naïve he had been all these years. He saw for the first time the truth behind his father's show of courage and sacrifice. He recognized the fear among the locals that Adel had earlier misunderstood for respect.

Yet, in his heart, Adel knew that this wouldn't change a thing. They would continue as a family and in few years, Adel would come to accept his father for what he was, even come to forgive him.

One day soon, Gholam would fade from his mind. The blood stained spectacles that Adel had found in the compound wouldn't anger him anymore. One day, Adel would toss those spectacles into a ditch and move on with his life, never thinking about them again.

Chapter 8

Fall 2010

Markos came home to find a message from Thalia on his phone. He hadn't called his mother in ages, and Thalia had sent him a reminder to do so.

Thalia had always been special to him. He had preserved the picture he had of her, standing on a beach in Tinos, with her back to the camera.

He first met her in the summer of 1967, when he was twelve years old. His mother, whose name was Odelia, had a childhood friend, Madeline, coming to visit her. She and her daughter would be staying with them for a few weeks. His mother had warned him that Madeline had a daughter who was attacked by a dog once. This had left a scar. Markos was expected to be polite and not stare.

Madeline was married to a wealthy, older man, Andreas Gianakos. Odelia was a school teacher and lived in a modest house with her son. The day her friend was to arrive, Odelia had tidied the house and put on her best clothes. She picked them up from the ferry port of Tinos, and Markos greeted them at the door when they arrived.

The first time Markos saw Thalia, Madeline's daughter, she had a mask around the lower half of her face. She stood behind her mother who was a beautiful woman with auburn hair, long legs and lots of makeup.

Madeline talked endlessly as soon as she entered through the door. Thalia was content to stand behind her mother in silence. On Madeline's insistence, she greeted Markos with a hello. Her rasping voice felt like a current and Markos couldn't stop staring at the mask draped around her mouth.

Later, Odelia asked Markos to carry a tray of tea to the bedroom occupied by Madeline and Thalia. As he entered, Markos caught Thalia's reflection in the mirror. She had her back to him and her scarf lay abandoned on the dressing table. Markos dropped the tray in shock. There were no words to describe it. It wasn't a scar. The dog had *eaten* her face.

Markos dreaded the weeks that he had to spend with Thalia in the same house. The sound of her voice gave him goose bumps. She ate noisily, always dropping bits of food from her mouth. She had to drink all liquids through a straw.

While Thalia hardly ever spoke, perhaps because she understood the way people reacted to her voice, her mother would never stop talking. She narrated fascinating stories about her travels to different parts of the world. Markos would enjoy listening to her.

One day, while the four of them were sitting together, Madeline told Markos that his mother had been her savior when they were young.

"It was my father," she said, "He would hit me all the time. I would always come running to Odie and take shelter in this very house. One day the beatings got out of control, and I ran to Odie, bleeding from my tongue, a patch of hair ripped from my scalp. Odie was furious. She walked out of the house, taking along her father's hunter rifle. She was going to end this once and for all, she told me. She walked into my house and pointed the rifle to my father's face. She threatened to shoot him the next time he raised his hand on me. That was it. My father never hit me again."

As Madeline finished her story, Markos looked at his mother in awe. She had never told him. He knew her mother had always been fierce. Always trying to protect and rescue the weak.

Odelia turned towards Thalia and tried to strike a conversation with her. Her replies were curt until she realized that she shared a common interest for science and knowledge with Odelia. That was the beginning of the special relationship that Odelia and Thalia would later go on to share.

On most days, Thalia and Markos were left to spend time together while Odelia and Madeline caught up on each other's life.

One day, while walking together through town, Markos caught sight of a camera on the window of a shop.

"Looks like a C3 Argus. Best selling camera in the world," Thalia said

Markos was surprised with her knowledge about cameras.

Thalia looked at Markos, "Your mother told me you wanted to be a photographer."

Markos shrugged, “I do. But I’ve never clicked a photograph in my life.”

Thalia looked at him with softened eyes that he imagined was her way of smiling “Maybe we can try building a camera for you to use.”

The next day, Thalia and Markos sat together in his upstairs bedroom, building a camera from scratch. They could hear Madeline talking to Odelia in whispers.

“I bet she’s talking about Andreas. They had a big fight,” Thalia said, “He has always been nice to me though. He’s a decent man.”

Once the camera was built, Markos and Thalia walked to the beach to click his first photograph. The sea was a beautiful blue, it looked perfect.

“All we need now is a subject.” Markos said, looking at Thalia.

On Markos’ insistence, she reluctantly agreed to pose for the picture, on condition that she would have her back to the camera.

She walked towards the sea and adjusted her hair so that the bands of her mask didn't show. Markos looked into the camera box; he could see Thalia's hair, the rocks around her, even a little tugboat at a distance. He counted till one twenty before dropping the shutter.

That picture, his first photograph, would prove to be one of his most precious possessions. The picture would accompany him through all his travels.

He would carry it with him to Rome, where his Italian girlfriend would question him about the girl in the picture. He would later find the picture in a bush, a corner of it burnt.

He would carry it to India, where he would one day wake up in a hospital bed, robbed of everything he had on him. The thieves had only left behind the photograph. The boy in the bed next to his, Manaar, would be unexplainably attracted to the picture. Perhaps it was the sea. He had probably never seen the sea in his life. Manaar would hold the picture to his chest, drawing comfort from it and he struck an unusual friendship with the boy.

Markos took some responsibility for the boy, who had been abandoned by his parents, but there was nothing he could do to prevent him from dying. Eventually, his experiences with Manaar and perhaps Thalia would influence his decision to apply to medical school.

He carried the photographs throughout his travels to Athens, Damascus, Cairo, and Munich. Eventually he carried the photograph with him to Kabul where it occupied a place of honor in his house.

One night, towards the end of summer, Madeline announced that she had to leave for Athens. She was an actress, and she was required to finish a shoot at Athens. Thalia was to stay with Markos and his mother for a few weeks while Madeline finished her work.

She could be home tutored by Odelia for a while, Madeline had suggested. That way Thalia wouldn't have a problem if she resumed school a little later.

Later that night, Thalia confided in Markos that Madeline was having an affair with the director of the movie. She also told him about Madeline's first husband,

Dorian and his giant dog, Apollo. Markos didn't have to ask to know that Apollo was the dog that had attacked her.

Years later, as their friendship grew, Thalia also told Markos about her plastic surgery that had gone terribly wrong. It had almost killed her and left her face even more distorted than it was before. She had decided that she wasn't going to ever try and fix her face after that.

The day that Madeline left, Odelia sat down with Thalia and told her that she was not required to wear her mask anymore. Markos realized then what his mother had known for weeks. The mask had been more for Madeline than Thalia. She wore it to save her mother from embarrassment.

When school resumed a few days later, Markos didn't attend. He instead chose to be homeschooled by his mother along with Thalia so that she wouldn't feel lonely.

When the people on the island started gossiping about Thalia's injury, it made Odie furious. She decided that Thalia was going to attend school, without her mask. The students at the school were always fearful of Odie and when she threatened them into treating Thalia with decency, they had no choice but to obey. After that day, Thalia never wore a mask again.

News about Madeline reached them several months later, from Thalia's step father, Andreas. She had run away with the director of her film. Madeline would never come back for her. Thalia had known this all along. Andreas offered to enroll Thalia in a private school and pay for her education. Thalia chose instead to stay with Odie and Markos.

Years passed. Markos moved to Athens to complete his medical degree and then to Kabul as a plastic surgeon. Thalia had stayed with Odie.

Markos called his mother from Kabul after receiving the voicemail from Thalia. He hadn't spoken to her in a while

Over the phone, Markos filled his mother in on Nabi's letter and Pari's visit to Kabul. She had come in the summer and stayed in the house for a week. At the end of her visit, she carried back with her Suleiman's sketch pads, Nila's poems, and Nabi's letter.

Markos promised his mother that he would come home soon. It had been two years since his last visit.

That winter, around Christmas, Markos travelled to Tinos. Thalia picked him up from the ferry port.

Back at home, Markos looked around at his unfamiliar surroundings. The house had changed over the years that he had been away. Markos didn't feel like he was a part of it anymore. It felt strange. He thought about all the moments that he had missed; precious moments with his mother who had been sick for several months. Thalia had taken care of her instead. She had been a daughter to Odie and a sister to Markos.

Markos tiptoed into the bedroom where is mother was fast asleep. She had lost a lot of weight. He noticed a bag of diapers and a walking stick by her bed.

At the corner of the room, he noticed a digital picture frame. Markos looked at it for a while before he realized that the pictures flashing on the frame were his photographs. They were photographs that he had clicked when he was travelling the world. He always sent a copy of these pictures to Thalia. She had kept them, even after all these years.

On the wall was a newspaper clipping. It was an interview that Markos had done in Kabul about his humanitarian work. In the center was a group photo of him, Nabi, Amra, Roshi, and a few other children. Thalia told him that his mother had found the article on the internet. She would look him up on the web every day.

After Odelia woke up, Markos tried questioning her about her sickness. She dismissed him. She could take care of herself, Odelia had said. Markos had always known his mother to be fierce and strong. She would never want to be a burden on anybody.

As they drank coffee, Odelia looked at Markos with soft eyes, "I worry for you, living in Kabul, but you make me proud."

All his life, that was all Markos ever wanted; to make his mother proud.

The next morning, the three of them sat in the balcony to witness the solar eclipse that had gotten everyone in Tinos excited. They looked up at the crescent shaped sun, and Thalia asked Odelia to open her hands, palms up. She placed a square of cut glass on Odelia's hand, and they watched as a crescent rainbow appeared.

Odelia beamed and looked at it in wonder. A wave of guilt and regret washed over Markos. He was fifty-five years old. He had never been around to watch his mother grow old, to take care of her when she was sick. Maybe it was too late to fix his relationship with his mother, but he had to try.

He reached out and held his mother's hand in his.

Chapter 9

Winter 2012

As a child, Pari had a little game that she and her father would play every night. After tucking her into bed, Abdullah would sit by her side and pluck the bad dreams out of her head. He would look for the bad dreams at her forehead, behind her ears, at the back of her head. He would remove them with a popping sound and place them in an imaginary bag. Then, he would give her a happy dream. He was a good storyteller, and he would make up a happy one. "You'll dream of this today," he would say.

Some nights, Pari would pull out the bad dreams from her Baba's head and give him a happy dream. The dream she would give him was always the same. Her Baba and his sister were lying below an apple tree, drifting in and out of sleep. It was a peaceful afternoon, and the sun warmed their faces and hands.

Pari was a lonely child. Eventually, she started finding companionship in an imaginary friend. She imagined a twin, also named Pari, with light green eyes, dark hair, and long lashes. She and Abdullah's little sister,

Pari, would do everything together. They would study, play, and sleep together. No one knew about Pari's childish games with her imaginary friend. She kept it a secret.

Even though Pari grew out of having an imaginary friend, she never stopped being lonely. By the time she was in junior high, she began longing for the freedom that most girls her age enjoyed. She wasn't allowed to try out for the swim team or the volleyball team, and she spent her summers helping her father around the restaurant. Abdullah insisted that she take Farsi lessons on Tuesday afternoons and Koran lessons on Sundays. It was important for him that his daughter remained in touch with her roots. Without them, she had no identity, he would say.

Then one day, Pari received an admission letter from an art institute in Baltimore. She had sent them her portfolio, and they had agreed to give her a full scholarship. It was her biggest achievement. She could be an artist; she could build a career around something she loved dearly.

For Abdullah, it was a terrifying thought; his daughter living alone in a faraway city. He tried to convince her to wait for a couple of years and reapply. Her mother, he said, would be unhappy with Pari gone.

Pari could see the fear in her Baba's eyes. She knew it wasn't for her mother, it was for him. He feared losing her. Pari loved her father dearly. She understood that his unreasonable fear came from his experiences as a child. He didn't want to lose her the way he had lost his sister. Pari knew that her relationship with her father would always be controlled by what had happened to Abdullah's sister. It was an incident that had happened decades ago, but it would always echo through her life.

Still, Pari needed to go. She wouldn't get an opportunity like this one again.

A few months later, just before Pari was to fly to Baltimore, her mother was diagnosed with ovarian cancer.

Pari abandoned her plans for an education in art. It was a difficult time for her family, and she had to stay by her parents' side.

During the months that her mother was fighting cancer, Pari took her on a short trip to the Santa Cruz Mountains. Pari felt more at ease with her mother than her father. She didn't struggle with the same insecurities that her father had. They spent the afternoon lazing on a balcony outside the restaurant. Her mother recounted the first time she met Abdullah in Peshawar.

"There's something I've been meaning to tell you," her mother said. Pari could sense the seriousness in her voice.

"Abdullah has a half-brother in Pakistan named Iqbal. He lives in a refugee camp with his family. Abdullah has never been in touch with them, but he sends his brother money once every three months."

Pari was shocked. All these years, her father had never told her about the family he had left behind.

"Why are you telling me now?" she asked.

"I've been handling the finances for years now. You'll have to take over soon." Her mother looked at Pari with sad eyes, "You'll have to take care of your father. He's terrified of being abandoned. He'll lose his way without you."

It was the morning of Christmas Eve when her mother died in their home, in a hospital bed that Pari had set up in the guest bedroom. A few years later, Abdullah began losing his memory.

One day, Pari came home to find broken glass on the floor. The gas burner had been left on. She knew then that she could never leave her father alone. She worked as a transcriptionist, something that she could do from home, and she put her dreams on hold.

When she first got the call from Paris, Pari wasn't surprised. It was a call she had been expecting her whole life. The person on the phone asked for her father.

"Who's this?" Pari asked.

"I'm his sister," she replied.

They talked for an hour. Pari Wahdati told her that she knew nothing of her history until she recently received a letter left behind by her Uncle. She had flown to Kabul during the summer and visited Shadbagh, the village where she and Abdullah were born. She also mentioned Iqbal, her half-brother, and her attempts to find him in Kabul.

They decided that Pari would fly down to California to meet her brother, and a few weeks later, she was waiting at the airport for her namesake to pick her up.

When Pari first saw her aunt at the airport, she noticed the European elegance that she carried along with her and the strong French accent. It wasn't the little girl with dark hair and green eyes that Pari had imagined as a child. Pari Wahdati was a grey haired woman in her sixties. As they drove away from the airport, she confessed that she was anxious and nervous about meeting her brother. It had been fifty-eight years.

"Baba, you have a visitor," Pari told him when they arrived at the house. Her father was busy watching TV and didn't like being disturbed. Pari put the TV on mute, "I have a friend that I want you to meet," she said gently.

Pari Wahdati entered their home. She walked anxiously toward Abdullah and took the chair beside him, not taking her eyes off of him for a single moment.

"Hello, Abdullah. I'm Pari. It's so nice to see you."

Abdullah looked at her for a while, his face expressionless. A moment of silence followed, "You have an accent," he said

"I've lived in Paris."

"Ah! I've always wanted to take my wife there. Her name is Sultana. Maybe, we will someday soon. Once she recovers from her cancer," Abdullah had a problem remembering that Sultana was dead. Some days, he would get upset when he couldn't see her.

"Where is she? Take her to me," he would tell his daughter.

"What did you say your name was again?" Abdullah asked.

"Pari"

"You have the same name as my daughter."

"Can I ask you a question, Abdullah? Why did you give your daughter that name?" Pari hoped that Abdullah could remember something.

He shook his head, a little agitated. He murmured something in Farsi under his breath. Her daughter was about to remind him that their guest did not understand Farsi when Pari Wahdati stopped her.

"What was that Abdullah? Can you say it out loud?" Abdullah hesitated, but he repeated himself without looking up:

"I know a sad little fairy

Beneath the shade of a paper tree,"

"There used to be a second verse, but Baba doesn't remember," Pari said.

Pari Wahdati let out a small laugh. In Farsi, she sang:

"I know a sad little fairy

Who was blown away by the wind one night."

Abdullah looked up at her, shaking his head. A small flash of recognition flashed through his eyes, but the moment passed.

Pari Wahdati spent the next month living with Abdullah and her daughter. She would take care of him, give him his pills, make him breakfast, and sit with him while he watched his TV shows.

She would tell her niece stories about her visit to Kabul. She told her about her attempts to find Iqbal. No one seemed to know what had happened to him, and even if they did, they seemed too nervous to tell her. She was worried that something terrible had happened to him.

The month passed, and it was time for Pari Wahdati to return to her home in Paris. A few months later, Abdullah's daughter, visited her aunt in France.

They were standing on the bridge in Avignon.

"How is he?" Pari Wahdati asked about her brother.

"He is worse than before."

Pari had to admit her father to a nursing home. His moments of lucidity had drastically reduced, and he was prone to having several fits of anger. Pari was incapable of taking care of him at home.

She was taken on a tour of the Memory Care Unit in the nursing home. She found the place suffocating and upsetting, but this was best for her father.

After he was admitted, she visited him often until she knew everyone on the staff by their first name. A day before she left for France, Pari went to see Abdullah.

He was sitting by the window in the recreation room, looking lost.

Pari told him about her trip. She was going to meet his sister and the rest of her family. They would meet in Paris, and then visit her daughter, Isabelle's vacation home in Provence. She would also be meeting Alain and Thierry. Isabelle and Alain had children too. It was going to be a big family reunion.

Abdullah looked at her, smiling in the same way that he smiled when she told him that she had been admitted to the College of Arts and Humanities in San Francisco. It was an indifferent smile. She knew that he couldn't understand her.

Before leaving, Pari ran her fingertips along his head, plucking out his bad dreams.

"Happy dreams, Baba. I'll see you soon."

Pari thought about her father now, as she and her aunt stood on the bridge. They talked about the family reunion. Pari thought about all of her cousins. She had spent most of her life feeling lonely. She had a family now, with cousins, nieces, and nephews.

"I have something to give you," Pari told her aunt.

After moving her father to the nursing home, Pari had spent days clearing her house. She finally worked up the nerves to clear out her parents rooms, get rid of all the old clothes. She repainted the house and converted her parent's room into a study.

While taking down the old suitcases, she had found a package in one of them. An envelope was taped to the package. It was written in Farsi: *For my sister, Pari.*

Pari brought the package to Paris to give to her aunt. Now as she handed it to her, Pari Wahdati took the package with trembling hands.

The letter inside the envelope was in Farsi. She asked her niece to read it for her. Abdullah's daughter took the letter and read it out loud:

"They tell me that I'm drowning and soon I won't have any memories left of us. Before I go, I want to leave this for you on the shore. I pray that you find it, sister. I want you to know that you were in my heart, even as I went under."

The letter was dated August 2007. It was the same month that Abdullah had been diagnosed.

Pari Wahdati tore open the package. Inside was an old tin tea box. The color of the box had faded over the years. She lifted the lid slowly. The interior of the box was stuffed with a huge collection of feathers of all colors and all sizes.

"Do you know what this means?" Pari asked her aunt.

She shook her head, "I have no memory of these feathers, but I do know what it means. It means that he never forgot me. Even after all these years. his love for me never faded."

That night, at the hotel, Pari watched her aunt as she slept. She slowly moved towards the bed and placed her hand on her aunt's forehead. She had a dream she wanted to give her.

It was a bright, sunny afternoon. The brother and sister were lying under a blossoming apple tree. They were young and carefree. His head rested on a root of the tree, hers on a coat that he had folded for her. Pari watched her brother, and he made her feel safe and protected. Her eyes closed slowly, and she drifted off to sleep.

Final Recap

Khaled Hosseini's third best-selling novel is as intriguing as his previous books.

And the Mountains Echoed is divided into nine chapters and each chapter reads like a short story. Eventually, what the author creates is a web of lives in different parts of the world, connected across generations.

The story of Abdullah and Pari sets the foundation of the book- Two siblings shared an extraordinary bond and were separated from each other at a young age.

As the book bounces from one character to the next, the reader is pulled into a complicated labyrinth of intertwined stories: the strained relationship between two sisters, the life of a servant in Kabul, an American Afghani suffering from survivors guilt, a suicidal and alcoholic mother with her daughter, the life of a Greek humanitarian working in Afghanistan, and the story of the young son of a jihadist.

The story ends with Abdullah and Pari's reunion, decades after they were separated, in far from ideal circumstances, where Abdullah cannot remember her.

Critical Review

Khaled Hosseini's new novel has for the most part been well received by critics. His writing skills have only improved since his first book, *The Kite Runner*, which was also a best seller.

The New York Times has great things to say about Hosseini's gift with storytelling: *"Mr. Hosseini's narrative gifts have deepened over the years, enabling him to anchor firmly the more maudlin aspects of his tale in genuine emotion and fine-grained details."*

The emotionally gripping novel keeps the reader spell bound even after the last page is turned. Los Angeles Times called the book *"painfully sad but also radiant with love."*

In the words of Washington Post critic, Marcela Valdes, *"It's hard to do justice to a novel this rich in a short review. There are a dozen things that I still want to say — about the rhyming pairs of characters, the echoing situations, the varied takes on honesty, loneliness, beauty, and poverty; the transformation of emotions into physical ailments."*

Unlike Hosseini's previous books, *And the Mountains Echoed* has been written like a series of short stories. Though unique and fascinating, there have been mixed reviews about the pattern that the book follows. The Toronto Star calls this *"the novel's most defining feature and it's most exasperating conceit."*

One flaw that has been pointed out within the book is the excessive melodrama. In the words of The New York Times, *"Mr. Hosseini shamelessly uses contrivance and cheesy melodrama to press every sentimental button he can."*

The climax, as with all of Hosseini's books, is not the perfect happy ending, but is not an entirely unhappy ending, either. In the words of The Telegraph, *"in the closing section, Hosseini pulls off his usual – impressive – trick of breaking your heart and leaving you smiling."*

If you enjoyed A Brief Read of And the Mountains Echoed, maybe you can work in some time to read the original. If there's a book that you'd like to see in A Brief Read, let us know!

Visit us on Amazon or ABriefRead.com!

Like us on Facebook for special promotions!

Made in United States
North Haven, CT
15 February 2022